INO INYAYA YENHAMBA

THE NUMBER STORY

SMALL BOOK ONE

ENGLISH - SHONA

Numbers Teach Children Their Number Names

written and illustrated by

MISS ANNA

Early Reader Edition of *The Number Story 1*
Bronze Medal Winner, 2016 Wishing Shelf Book Award

Library of Congress Control Number: 2018902040

Names: Miss Anna, author.
Title: Number story : numbers teach children their number names / Miss Anna.
Description: Portland, OR: Lumpy Publishing, 2018.
Identifiers: ISBN 978-1-945977-78-7 | LCCN 2018902040
Summary: The pictures and rhymes present stories which introduce numbers 0-10.
Subjects: LCSH Numeration—English--Shona--Pictorial works--Juvenile literature. | BISAC JUVENILE NONFICTION /
Languages: English--Shona
Classification: LCC QA141.3 .M57 2018 | DDC 513—dc23

Publisher: Lumpy Publishing
Website: www.missannabooks.com
Email: missanna@missannabooks.com

Paperback: ISBN 978-1-945977-78-7
Printed in the U.S.A.   1 3 5 7 9 10 8 6 4 2

Unoda kudzidzi mazita
emanhamba here?

It is very easy and a lot of fun!

Kudzidza uku kunonankidza
uye hakuna kuoma!

Say-along our little jingle

Imba nesu kachimbo kedu aka!

starting from Number One!

Tichatangira kubva panhamba yechiposhi!

1

ONE looks like my one finger.

POSHI

yakafanana nechigumwe changu.

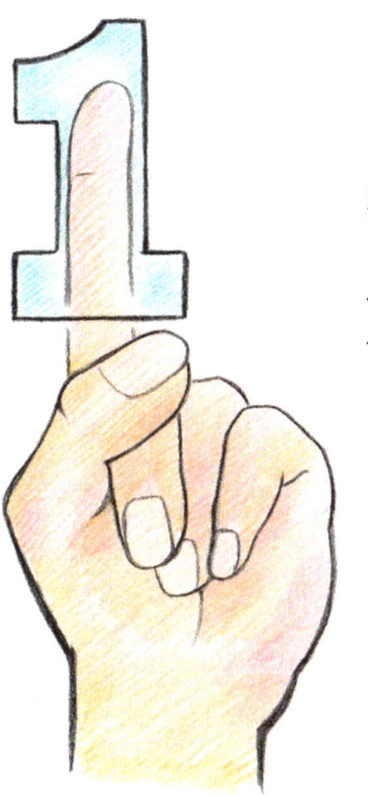

1
ONE!
POSHI!

2

TWO   trails a tail.

PIRI

inotevera muswe.

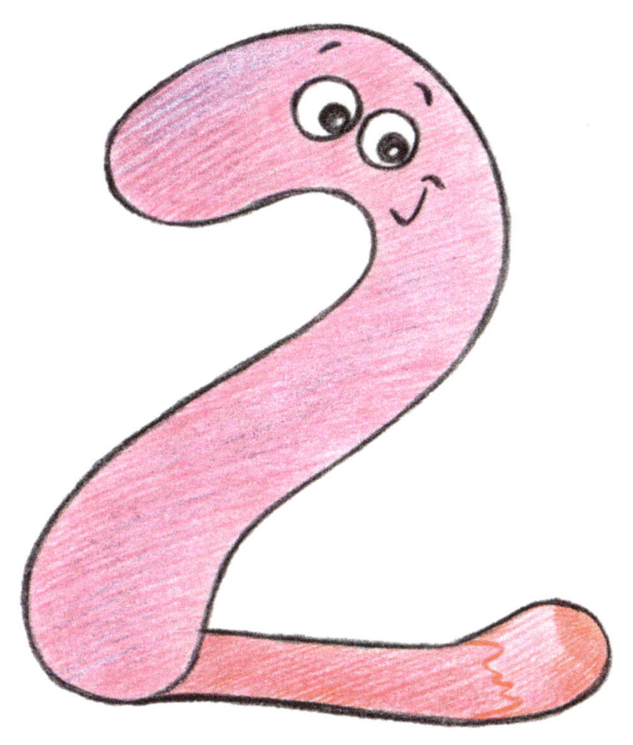

A TAIL! MUSWE!

3

THREE   has bumps.

TATU

yakaita sechuru.

Tarisa churu chine ruvara rwemashizha icho!

4

FOUR   carries a sail.

INA

ine chikepe.

4

A SAIL!

CHIKEPE ICHO!

5

FIVE   is a racing track.

SHANU

iri mutsara wekumhanya.

VROOM
VROOOM!
1

6

SIX   curves like a snail.

TANHATU

inobhenda kunge hozhwa.

A SNAIL!   HOZHWA IYO!

7

SEVEN   has a sharp angle.

NOMWE
ine kona rinocheka.

BE CAREFUL! IT'S SHARP!
Chenjera! Chinocheka!

8

E I G H T   is rollercoaster rails.

SERE

yakaita semuzeerere wenjanji.

YiPPEE!
YIPPEE!

NINE   is a bubble on a stick.

PFUMBAMWE
idenderedzwa remvura
riri pachitanda.

A BUBBLE!

DENDEREDZWA REMVURA IRO!

10

TEN   is an eye of a whale.

GUMI

iziso rimwe rehove huru.

HELLO! MHORO!

And
Ne
0
ZERO   is an empty pail.

ZERO
chigubhu chisina chinhu.

IT'S EMPTY!
Hamuna Chinhu!

Thank you for playing with us today.

We had a lot of fun too!

Totenda nekutamba nesu nhasi.

Tafara tose zvikuru!

We are your Number friends,
Zero to Ten,
Who will be here for you~
Tisu shamwari dzako dzemanhamba
Zero kusvika Gumi.
Ticharamba tiripano kana uchitida!

Bye-bye now!
See you again soon!
Sara mushe parizhino!
Tichaonana zvakare munguva
pfupi inotevera!

The Numbers are *SINGING* too!

To sing-a-long, look for Miss Anna Number Story
at your favorite music store like iTUNES.

MP3

Numbers 0-10
IDENTIFYING
& COUNTING

Numbers 11-20
& Ordinals

first, second, third...

Numbers 0-100
& Place Values

ones, tens, hundreds...

About Clocks
& Telling Time

hours, minutes, second

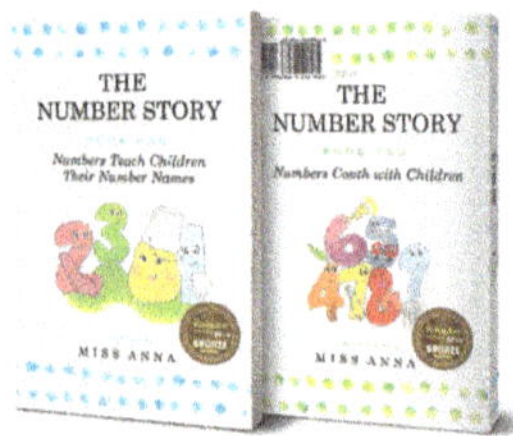

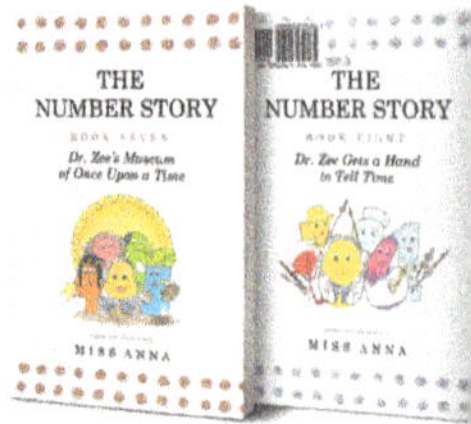

Number Story 1 & 2

isbn: 978-0-996216-48-7

Number Story 3 & 4

isbn: 978-1-945977-01-5

Number Story 5 & 6

isbn: 978-1-945977-06-0

Number Story 7 & 8

isbn: 978-1-949320-40-

For more Miss Anna books to love,
visit us at

w w w . m i s s a n n a b o o k s . c o m

Numbers are working hard all over the world!
Come Travel the World with Us!

www.ingramcontent.com/pod-product-compliance
Lightning Source LLC
Chambersburg PA
CBHW041100050726
47599CB00018B/2214